VARIETY TURNS

Christopher Arksey is a writer and voice actor. His poems have appeared in *Anthropocene, Full House Literary, Moist Poetry Journal, Porridge, Sledgehammer Lit, The York Journal*, and the Broken Sleep Books anthology *Companions of His Thoughts More Green: Poems for Andrew Marvell*. He lives in Hull with his wife and two sons.

© 2024 Christopher Arksey. All rights reserved; no part of this book may be reproduced by any means without the publisher's permission.

ISBN: 978-1-916938-01-4

The author has asserted their right to be identified as the author of this Work in accordance with the Copyright, Designs and Patents Act 1988

Cover designed by Aaron Kent

Edited by Aaron Kent

Typeset by Aaron Kent

Broken Sleep Books Ltd
Rhydwen
Talgarreg
Ceredigion
SA44 4HB

Broken Sleep Books Ltd
Fair View
St Georges Road
Cornwall
PL26 7YH

In their measured, quiet, honest way, these small poems carry a great weight of grief. Their craft lies in knowing how much can be stated obliquely, with a light touch and the unexpected phrase, wittily, pleasurably. They pay tribute to the brave spirit of the dying with a bravery of their own, and together they constitute a monument that can be visited again and again, each time with undiminished freshness.
— **Christopher Reid**

In one of the powerful elegies of *Variety Turns*, Christopher Arksey finds random traces of his mother while time-travelling on Google Earth. Poring over them with rapt attention, he nevertheless knows 'not one of these /made a difference'. On the level of deep and sympathetic understanding, these are poems that very much do make a difference. A bedroom with a view of a cemetery, an insistent departed presence 'diminishing in full view', 'the most convincing /rendition of dying /I've ever seen' – no detail of Arksey's work is without its Hardyesque and robustly bittersweet melancholy. Out of wrenching loss he has made durable art, and poems that leave the reader both 'spent and roused'.
— **David Wheatley**

Christopher Arksey's *Variety Turns* allows unflashy, thoughtful elegies for his mother to make their point both quietly and effectively. There is a real sense of loss being worked through seriously and with dignity, which is sustained by careful choices of word and phrase. In 'Nil', Arksey catches mourners paying their respects: 'Some were all prayers. / While others warmed their chairs // in sniffled vigil and waited / for the next to take their places'; 'My singular loss / humbled by multiple thefts, / as each arrived and more left.' 'Last Words' builds a powerful sequence from laconic fragments: 'Every morning and night / the cemetery peeked over its height // of brick wall to check in on you'. In 'Actor', he catches the way we often fail to comprehend the reality of death, or shy away from its finality, conditioned as we are by fictional portrayals: 'The most convincing / rendition of dying / I've ever seen.'

Variety Turns is an impressive debut: a thirty-odd page sequence without flab or bluster. Arksey is not afraid to be serious, but is aware that craft is the best proof of sincerity. The poems are constructed with both care and feeling that never rings hollow, though the verse avoids the pitfalls of calling attention to itself and the skill with which it has been so artfully assembled.
— **Cliff Forshaw**

The poems in *Variety Turns* are controlled, expressive and affecting. Arksey can be playful and clever but his project is a serious one, and these poems are deeply felt and finely made.
— **Hilary Menos**

i.m. June Clutterbuck, née Dillon
3 July 1955 – 27 June 2016

CONTENTS

Tough Guy	11
Drama	12
Ceremony	13
Tried Praying	14
The View	15
Nil	16
Last Words	17
Vigil	24
Actor	25
Trainer	26
Wake	27
Amateur Gardener	28
The First Summer	30
The Laugh	31
Song for June 2016	32
Grief	33
Myth	34
Portfolio	35
Notes and acknowledgements	39

Variety Turns

Christopher Arksey

Broken Sleep Books

TOUGH GUY

It snowed that year. I know because I've studied
the camcorder footage that was unearthed,
trying to pick you out of the muddied
jostle but finding you uncaptured,
just out of shot. I imagine how the mud
dug into your soles as you stampeded
the field, piled into the row in front and vaulted
the rusted bars of the iron gate. How it thawed
at the edges of the ditch you dunked
in, steeped waist-high in its colour and cold.
How it bloodied, not far from the barbed
wire crawl where a few got their head
and shoulders nicked flinching from a live round.
How it smeared thick the tunnels most travelled,
the surest exits. How it pulped into matted
heaps of burnt hay and dung, clogged
the braids of ropes you clung to, filled
your nostrils, ears and fingernails, blathered
your numbered white T-shirt, and printed
a hand on the cup of tea that steamed
the lens and scorched your lip at the race's end.

DRAMA

How I wish I could've been there to see
the look on your father's face as you gave
him the news. You were not going to be
the actor you dreamed of that he forbade,
despite your visceral performances.
No, you were going to get a proper
job. "Mental health nurses aren't real nurses,"
he said. He should know; he was a porter
at the infirmary. It was a slight
you couldn't miss, choosing psychiatry.
Just enough to appease him, but not quite.
Still, what could've been: university,
auditions, rejections, your first big break,
all the roles you wanted you couldn't take.

CEREMONY

After peeling a banana
you'd chop it widthways,
butter two white slices
and arrange the pieces
four by four.
Then pat and press,
and with a clink of knife
cut corner to corner,
bring the first half
to your mouth without
needing a plate.
If I train my ears
I can bring it all back:
the rhythmic jaw click
as you chew a bite intact,
the muffled clunk
of blade on board
slicing many parts to one,
the bread unbuttered,
the skin tears sutured,
the banana now whole,
turning spotless,
green, unripened
in the fruit bowl.

TRIED PRAYING

While time-travelling
in Google Street View,
I spot your *trypraying*
sticker. A year or two
uproots the bay
tree and plants a new
For Sale sign, while pansies
bloom in the entrance.
Not one of these
made a difference.

THE VIEW

At least you got the room beside the yard.
At least, among paving slabs, rockeries
of hardy shrubs were there for your last view.
But through other windows lining the square,
I saw chairs all angled to face the beds,

sills littered with mugs, and the backs of heads.
Untalkative, like us. So this is where
you're put when they've done all they can for you;
unhooked and wheeled away with skilful ease.
At least you got the room beside the yard.

NIL

As each left more arrived.
    Old friends, colleagues, church
regulars joined to say goodbye.
    I gave up my seat and perched

on the windowsill, edging
    in and out of last conversations.
A one-time congregation
    of sorts. Some dredging

holiday stories and office jokes
    to keep it light, stifling croaks
of laughter. Some were all prayers.
    While others warmed their chairs

in sniffled vigil and waited
    for the next to take their places.
Your life's work concentrated
    to one room. In their faces

flashed sides I'd not seen in you.
    Roles outside of mum and wife,
the ones that rounded up your life,
    were now diminishing in full view:

loyal companion, beloved boss,
    true believer. My singular loss
humbled by multiple thefts,
    as each arrived and more left.

LAST WORDS

       1
"You're handsome, you're clever,
you're funny."

To this, your perfectly cadenced farewell,
the best reply I could muster:

"You're not too bad yourself."

A feeble comeback, now I think of it,
clutched at between tears

and choked out as I fumbled for your hand.

2

When the nurse asked why
you took your mask off, you said, dryly:

"Because I can."

Composed in your resolve, even then,
not to give death the satisfaction,

but to stare down its indifference
with your own slice of nonchalance:

lock-jawed, bleary-eyed,
a look that says just kill me.

3

Without a sure closer I was happy with,
I resolved to be cautious.

Avoid the sombre goodbyes.
Tap into the reserves

of thought-terminating clichés.
Chat about the day as it unfolds.

Plan the future as if you're a part of it.

Keep saying hello.

4

Cupping my jaw in your hands
and smiling under your mask,

you managed a crackled, breathy:

"I like it."

You weren't to know
that was the longest shave of my life,

crying unguarded in the mirror
as I stop-started the shaver.

5

There was a pause,
and then you came out with it:

"I won't get to see you all grow up."

My body answered with a silent, heaving sob
that shrugged off my best efforts to stop.

My older brother's stabling grip
of my shoulder replied:

Youth is on our side
but also against us.

6

I'm glad I missed your call
and recorded your voicemail

before its 30 saved days were up.
It may not be studio quality

but it's a preserve all the same,
and the only one I have

that memory can't warp.

"I've got the bay tree in the car,
but there's more to come."

7

Every morning and night
the cemetery peeked over its height

of brick wall to check in on you
through your bedroom

window. A dealbreaker for
some, to neighbour

with the dead, but not for you.
Drawing the curtains each day to view

one another: poised, peaceful, green.

"And *they* don't bother me."

VIGIL

Perhaps sensing the choke
in the atmosphere,
or to remind us you were
still breathing, you'd crack
a fart across the air.
Impossible to unhear,
it yielded like a kept joke
within hours. And now years,
in their infinite mercy,
have amplified its comedy.

ACTOR

With digital precision
the hourly injections
lulled you into half-sleep,
halving you each
day till your eyes shut
and wouldn't open,
and you stopped
responding to voice or touch.
I left for home feeling
you'd already gone.
Not you in that bed
but an alternate,
with eyelids closed for the last,
skin grey-cool,
veins branched.
The lung-wheezing,
brain-panting final moments.
The most convincing
rendition of dying
I've ever seen.

TRAINER

You were formidable by all accounts,
though I've heard only one.

When asked by the pastor
on what she meant, your sister,

also a nurse, let slip a knowing expression
followed by nodding exclamations

that called for nothing
else, but which I crudely took to mean:

"And if you give me shit,
I'll *really* let you have it."

Words I never heard you use,
of course, and a characteristic you

characteristically played down.

WAKE

You said not the pub.
So we went to the pub.
Not in ignorance,
nor defiance,
nor want of that wry,
delicious punchline
you'd have enjoyed,
but because
we didn't know
where else to go.

AMATEUR GARDENER

It's foolish of me
but I'm keeping you alive as the bay tree.

I have you standing guard
in the sheltered front garden,

confined to a cracked pot
too small to root,

but leafing larger every year;
shading what goes on in here.

When your leaves yellow, I pick them off,
let fall to the breathing moss

that has grassed-in the trunk:
a haphazard clump of mulch.

Afraid you'll prosper
or die back altogether,

I stop myself from digging deep
and potting up.

Best not to break the pot
and prise you out:

soils, cells, vitals,
root ball and all.

And talking to you,
like all sensible gardeners do,

seems out of the question;
a fool's experiment in suppression.

No, better to prune and pine
and bide my time

watering till you bubble and overflow.
Ridiculous, I know.

THE FIRST SUMMER

Every summer from now on
is the one just gone.

I never finish anything. The half-
painted fence stays proof
of a hack and his odd jobs.

I learn and forget the Latin names for plants.
My *Sambucus Nigra* is *Black Beauty*,
That Beauty, That Elderberry, That There.

I defend the bay tree from caterpillar
attacks. First with fatherly patience,
second brute force, third all-out surrender.

I steal time talking about gardening.
My gung-ho fervour dries up
long before the first frosts.

THE LAUGH

It was like you'd surfaced after a spell
underwater; spent and roused at the same time,
breathless towards the inevitable
big-reveal of your long-delayed punchline.

Then you let fly — the laugh of someone twice
your size — with such potency it rocked your frame
and sent you seeking my arm for balance,
stopping short of doubling over from the strain.

Only this soundless record of it exists.
And I forget the joke, but I've got the gist.

SONG FOR JUNE 2016

after The Clash

Should I stay or should I go?
Or should I let life course naturally,
trust that when the time is right I'll know?

But wait too long and indecision can grow.
Even the doctor can't say with certainty
if this is the day she will stay or she will go.

Each morning the news on the radio
confronts the will of a slim majority.
So the time *was* right — how did we not know?

While on the TV, a knockout show:
everything rests on the next taker's penalty
to decide who will stay and who will go.

It was only a year ago
she was bold and beaming at our wedding ceremony.
When the time is right, she said, you'll know.

Eleven months later, aglow
with pride, she held our newborn baby.
Let him stay, she said, don't make him go.
And when the time was right, he let her know.

GRIEF

Indescribable,
though I've tried.
Failing in my usual
way of stumped silence
or inarticulate babble.
The best I can offer:
a permanent resident,
neither seen nor heard,
though their presence
is felt everywhere.

MYTH

A bee can carry its own weight in pollen, and still fly.
Clumsily, and with great strain. But it can, and it will, fly.

And yet the myth persists: *It goes against every*
law of physics that a bee should be able to fly.

Is it that a plausible lie can be easier to live with?
Or the comfort in knowing something so leaden can still fly?

That if we could only ignore life's drag
we too might, in spite of our lack of skill, fly.

Why else would I tell my sons their grandma lives
in the clouds — that only through dying was she able to fly?

Then in the next breath offer to visit her grave; say this
is where she'll land to rest, listen — and off again she'll fly.

Watch as disbelief melts to wonder on their faces as they
imagine being both of the earth and the sky. One day we'll fly

like she does: bumbling, the weight of past lives in tow.
Look up, boys. See Clutterbuck, Arksey, Dillon fly.

PORTFOLIO

In full trainee nurse uniform,
regulation bob and flat shoes,
gurning like that duck-faced
doll you grew up with.

*

Now in scruffs and rigging
gloves, splitting concrete,
lugging bricks, shying
away from the camera.

*

Behatted, fresh from
graduation pomp.
And before that,
a speeding ticket.

*

A sun-glared smile
with pair of pants on head:
your makeshift tieback
for the bracing wind.

*

Calf-deep in the sea
casting a shadow behind you,
turning the water as blue
as its deepest depths.

*

In the distance, above your
head, two dogs: one submerged
up to the neck, the other
in the shallows watching on.

*

Frazzled by work and sun.
The shot you wish were never
taken, of which I now have three:
standard, zoom, double zoom.

*

Brandished in '70s saturation:
big glasses, bigger hair, all teeth.
One last snap before you enter
the world proper.

*

Here, your effortless
magnetism is made flesh:
a picnic with the family,
each body facing yours.

*

Half a second later,
startled by an unfamiliar
sound, the dog leaps from
your back and exits the frame.

*

It's as if you'd beaten
gravity at its own game.
Sprung from a trampoline,
never to come down again.

NOTES AND ACKNOWLEDGEMENTS

Tough Guy was said to be the 'toughest race in the world'. It was first staged in 1987, and held on a 600-acre farm in Perton, Staffordshire. The race comprised a cross country run followed by an obstacle course, also known as the Killing Fields.

'Tough Guy' and 'Myth' were published by *Anthropocene*; 'Wake' by *Sledgehammer Lit*; and 'The Laugh' by *The Friday Poem*. 'Ceremony' appeared in *Full House Literary* under its previous title, 'In Reverie'.

Thank you to Christopher Reid, David Wheatley, Cliff Forshaw and Hilary Menos for their kind and generous endorsements. To Christopher, David and Cliff for their teaching and encouragement all those years ago. To Cliff for his friendship and guidance. And to Aaron Kent for his care, skill and patience in bringing this book to publication.

Kat, Freddie, Bertie and the rest of my family, thank you all for your love and support.

LAY OUT YOUR UNREST

Milton Keynes UK
Ingram Content Group UK Ltd.
UKHW010831210124
436385UK00002B/19

9 781916 938014